D0551426

How
Wales
Beat the Mighty
All Blacks

To my son, Michael, and my daughter, Helena.
Thanks for all the joy and inspiration. – James

To Mum and Dad. Thank you for all your love,
support and patience. – Carys

First impression: 2021

Cover design: Y Lolfa
Cover image: Carys Feehan

ISBN: 978-1-80099-034-0

Published and printed in Wales on paper from well-maintained forests by
Y Lolfa Cyf., Talybont, Ceredigion SY24 5HE
e-mail ylolfa@ylolfa.com
website www.ylolfa.com
tel 01970 832 304

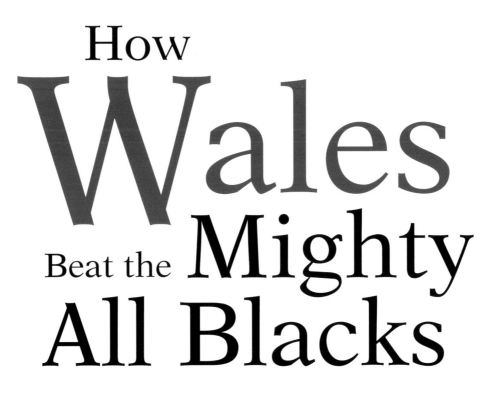

How Wales
Beat the Mighty
All Blacks

James Stafford

Illustrated by Carys Feehan

Cardiff, Wales. Autumn of 1905.

This is Mr Erith Gwyn Nicholls. The great newspapers of the day usually just called him Gwyn, but occasionally they called him Mr Nicholls. When the people talked about him, though, they called him 'Prince'.

Why? You see, so elegant, fast, skilful and strong was Mr Nicholls on the rugby field, he was nicknamed the 'Prince of Centres'. For almost ten glorious years he had helped his country to many famous wins, including not one, but three Triple Crowns. A Triple Crown was claimed when one of Wales, England, Scotland or Ireland beat all of the others in a single season. Back then, it was the biggest prize in rugby.

But in the autumn of 1905, Mr Nicholls was a very content, and terribly busy, former rugby player.

Back in these distant days, rugby players were not paid a penny. Even the great superstars like Mr Nicholls still had to make a living. After suffering so many bumps, bruises, knocks and whacks during his illustrious career, Mr Nicholls had hung up his boots. The fans and newspapers of the day pleaded with him to keep guiding Wales to championships, but glory didn't feed his family.

Mr Nicholls was firm. "I'm retired," he would tell dozens of people every single day when they asked him when he was coming back. "I've a laundry business to run and no time for rugby."

While Mr Nicholls was running a successful business, 11,000 miles away on the other side of the world, something rather special was happening. A new rugby team had been formed in New Zealand – a place known as the 'Land of the Long White Cloud'. Their nation was at the time a small (but proud) corner of the British Empire. These young men of New Zealand were gathering for what would be one of the greatest sporting adventures ever known. Wishing to challenge the might of Europe and North America, they were set to sail across the oceans to combat the best sides the rugby world could offer.

These men were a fearsome sight. Ginormous, tough, athletic, quick, brave and cunning, they burned with a passion to show the world how mighty their 'little land' was. A daunting 35 games lay ahead of them. But before the 'Kiwis' (nicknamed after their national bird) set sail on a sea voyage that would take them 42 long days, the Prime Minister of New Zealand called them together and gave them a fiery speech: "We must show those back in the British Isles, which some call the Mother Country, exactly what we are made of. And the greatest of those teams is Wales. More than anyone, this is the nation that we must overcome to prove our worth!"

Even as their ship navigated the seas, the New Zealanders never ceased in their efforts to be the best. They jogged and sprinted on deck, they boxed one another, they helped shovel heavy heaps of coal into the giant furnaces that powered the huge steam liner, they scrummaged with each other and did everything they could to keep in tip-top shape. By the time they arrived in England to play their first game, they were like wild beasts, ready to be unleashed upon the world.

Their first encounter was with the rugby men of Devon, twice English County Champions in the previous few years. The New Zealanders, clad head to toe in fearsome black, stormed into action. Led by their strapping captain Dave Gallaher, the 'underdog' All Blacks tore their hapless opponents apart. In these olden times a try was worth just three points. Yet the New Zealanders triumphed by 55 to 4!

The local spectators and journalists could scarcely believe their eyes. As news of the trouncing spread across the land by telegram, many simply refused to believe it was true. Some newspapers 'corrected' the score to show Devon had won 55-4, as they could not imagine a team from the far end of the world could win so heavily in the land that had invented rugby.

But soon the whole of England, Scotland, Ireland and Wales knew the score was no mistake. Next, the terrifying men in black pounded the pride of Cornwall by 41-0. Then Bristol fell by the exact same score. Next came 32 points to nil against Northampton. Then 28-0 over Leicester. On and on it went. The English teams simply had no answer. One famous rugby writer asked if it was humanly possible to improve on the astounding feats these sons of the British Empire could perform.

Back in Wales, the stories of these mighty warriors from the Land of the Long White Cloud alarmed the country's rugby folk. Scouts were sent to England to study these mysterious men. The reports that came back only made them sound even more terrifying. Not only were they fitter, faster and bigger than British players, they scrummaged differently and had even invented a new position called a 'rover', who was half back and half forward. It seemed they were as cunning as they were brutal.

"The All Blacks are coming!" was the whisper on the lips of people all over Wales. "Whoever can stop them?"

"Not me," said Mr Nicholls. "I have a business to run and a family to feed."

As New Zealand continued to sweep all aside, nerves were fraying among the Triple Crown champions. Could even Wales stop this rugby machine? Without their greatest player, few gave them a chance.

"We need the Prince back!" screamed the Welsh newspapers.

"I can't help," answered Mr Nicholls. "I have a business to run and a family to feed."

The Kiwis, meanwhile, went on crushing all that came before them. 63-0. 44-0. 32-0. It felt like there was a darkness spreading all over the British Isles and no team could produce a spark of light to stop it.

But as he read the latest sensational news about the New Zealanders, Mr Nicholls's heart would beat a little faster. To face such a challenge and triumph, he thought, would surpass everything he had ever done in the red shirt of Wales.

"They call me the greatest," he thought to himself. "But how will I know I really am if I don't try to stop these mighty men?"

One cold winter morning, Mr Nicholls rose early. He had dreamt all night of the fearsome All Blacks and awoke in a sweat. Unable to get back to sleep, he got dressed and pulled on some soft leather training shoes. He opened the door and stepped into the bitterly cold dawn air. Closing his eyes, Mr Nicholls imagined himself once more in his beloved scarlet shirt, standing proudly on the sacred field of Cardiff Arms Park, Wales's hallowed national rugby ground. He recalled all the occasions on which the magical sound of thousands of Welsh fans singing songs of praise had inspired him and his team to great feats. He smiled to himself and then opened his eyes, blew on his fingers to warm them up, and ran into the morning fog.

The All Blacks were coming and Mr Nicholls was coming back.

When news spread that Mr Nicholls was back in training, there was a rush of excitement across the nation. From the docks of Cardiff to the mines of the Valleys, on the farms of west Wales and in the pulpits of the village chapels, the rugby resurrection of Mr Nicholls was on the lips of all.

Soon Mr Nicholls was again in the blue and black of Cardiff. He knew he had to make the most of every chance he had to get ready for the challenge that was coming. At first he was a little unsure, a little slow and a little short of breath. Many wondered if he had lost the magic that he once graced the fields of Wales with. But each week, he got a little faster, a little fitter and a little slicker.

But so did the All Blacks.

While Mr Nicholls got back in shape, the All Blacks comfortably swatted aside the challenges of Scotland, Ireland and England on three consecutive Saturdays. By the time they reached Wales, they had won 27 of 27 games. Nobody had even managed to score against them for seven matches. They had bagged an astonishing 801 points and allowed a measly 22. The newspapers wondered how many points they would pile up against little old Wales.

"The fathers and sons of Britain and Ireland are no match for this new breed of men," wrote one journalist. "We've gone soft here in the Mother Country. These fine specimens in the far corner of our British Empire breathe fresher air, eat better food and work harder on the open fields. No wonder we cannot compete. What chance have the Welsh? Of all the teams in these lands, they are the smallest. The Kiwi will eat the Dragon for breakfast."

Eventually the big week arrived. Mr Nicholls had been honoured with the captaincy of 'Gallant Little Wales'. Knowing that something special was required to combat the might of their opponents, Mr Nicholls did a very unusual thing for the time. He called the team together to have a special practice before the match. They had a clever idea on how to trick their opponents and wanted to practise it as much as possible beforehand.

On the afternoon before the clash, Mr Nicholls sat in his office alone, pondering what the next day would bring. He began to worry whether he had made a mistake. What if he was too old? Too slow? Why would he be able to stop what 27 other teams of younger men had failed to halt? Suddenly, a black cat wandered into the room and interrupted his thoughts.

"Hello," said Mr Nicholls. "A black cat! Are you a lucky or an unlucky omen?"

The cat licked its lips mischievously and purred. Smiling, Mr Nicholls gave it an affectionate stroke.

On 16th December 1905, the whole of Wales awoke to a cold, crisp winter's day. Tens of thousands of folk from across the land made their way to Cardiff. Almost 100 extra trains had been put on to meet demand. Some fans who had no money, like the striking miners of Monmouthshire, walked many miles over many days to be there. The docks in Cardiff closed early so working men could get to the Arms Park in time to queue for tickets. Those who couldn't get tickets climbed trees or paid to stand on top of horse-drawn carriages to get even the smallest glimpse of the arena where the two teams would do battle.

The newspapers declared it the 'Unofficial Championship of the World'. Almost nobody thought the men in scarlet had the slightest chance.

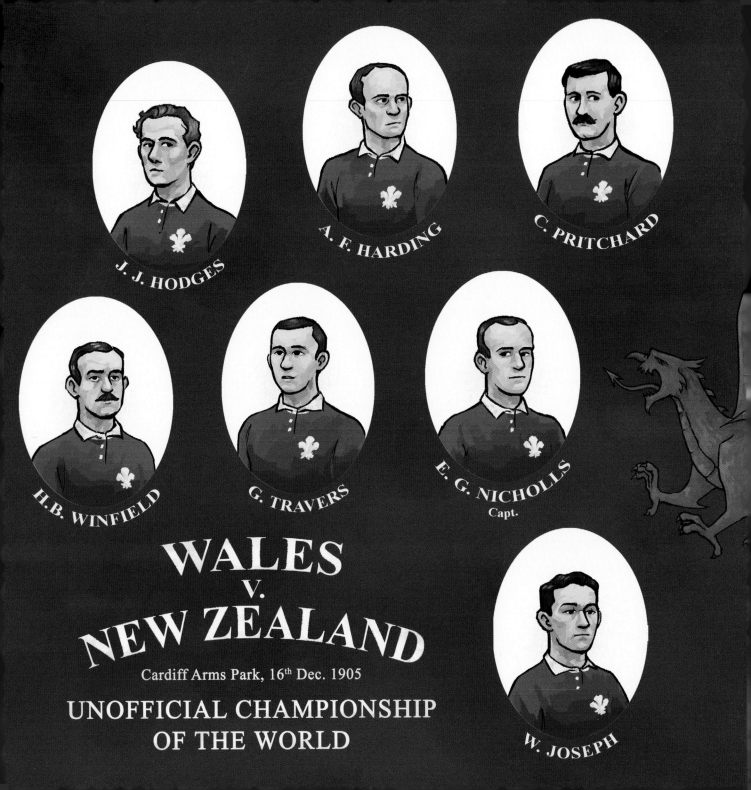

J. J. HODGES

A. F. HARDING

C. PRITCHARD

H.B. WINFIELD

G. TRAVERS

E. G. NICHOLLS
Capt.

W. JOSEPH

WALES
V.
NEW ZEALAND

Cardiff Arms Park, 16th Dec. 1905

UNOFFICIAL CHAMPIONSHIP
OF THE WORLD

Almost 50,000 people squeezed tightly into Cardiff Arms Park on that magical day. Just before the game, Mr Nicholls gathered his men around him. Having to speak loudly to be heard above the singing that vibrated through the stadium, the proud captain proclaimed:

"The eyes of the rugby world are on Wales today. It is up to us to prove that the Old Country is still capable of giving New Zealand a hard fight. We have already discussed tactics. So it only remains to me to appeal to you to be resolute in your tackling. Every man in possession must be put down, ball and all. As for the forwards, you already know what to do… Come on! Let's get out there!"

When the teams emerged on to the field of play, there was such a roar that the horses on the streets around the ground bolted in fright. All Blacks captain Dave Gallaher led his men in the awe-inspiring haka. It was a sight that no Welsh fan had ever witnessed before and the crowd gasped in wonder at this spine-tingling ritual. How could Wales respond to such a challenge?

As the crowd's hearty roar of approval for the haka faded away, little Welsh winger Teddy Morgan nervously cleared his throat and began to sing.

"Mae hen wlad fy nhadau yn annwyl i mi…"

He sang with all his heart and his teammates, inspired, took up the next line with him...

"Gwlad beirdd a chantorion, enwogion o fri…"

Slowly the crowd nearest the pitch, hearing the hearty singing of the players, joined in. Excitement and wonder rippled through the mass of people and soon 50,000 voices rang out:

"Gwlad! GWLAD! Pleidiol wyf i'm gwlad."

Such a thing had never happened at any sporting event ever before. The hairs on the back of each New Zealander's neck stood up straight. For the first time since they had set sail from their homeland months before, there was doubt in the minds of these supermen.

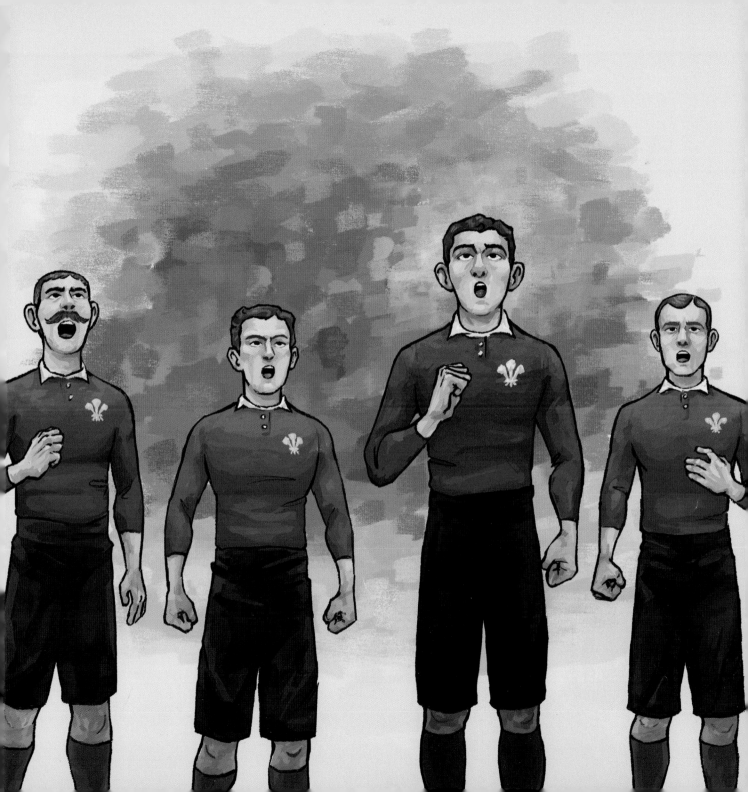

The match shuddered into life with a series of titanic collisions. Mr Nicholls made an early bone-crunching tackle on a tough Kiwi named James Hunter. As the two staggered back to their feet, Hunter, attempting to hide the pain he felt, snarled, "You're too old for this game — why don't you give up?"

Wales's tiny scrum half Dicky Owen, barely half the size of some of his opponents, was knocked clean out after some rough play. He rose up and was soon beaten down again and broke some ribs. But there were no replacements back then and so, shrugging his shoulders, he soldiered on bravely.

The spectators winced and wailed and roared as the teams bashed into each ferociously. Mr Nicholls, leading the way as captain, tackled another All Black star, lifting him back five metres and driving him to the ground. His men, who had begun to tire from the battle to keep out the relentless black waves of attackers, took inspiration from their 'old' leader and redoubled their efforts.

After thirty exhausting minutes, Wales earned a scrum, smack bang on the middle of the New Zealand 22. Mr Nicholls made a secret signal to his men. "This is our chance," he whispered to his half backs, Percy Bush and Dicky Owen. "Let's do what we practised this week."

The tough Welsh pack pushed hard and gave great ball for plucky Dicky Owen. The pocket rocket, ignoring his broken ribs, shot to his right, followed by Percy Bush and Mr Nicholls. The All Blacks defence moved like hungry lions, ready to pounce, and shadowed the trio across the field.

Suddenly, Owens threw an astonishing reverse pass back across the pitch to the expectant hands of Cliff Pritchard! A dash… a burst… and Pritchard was away. Just in time to avoid a tackling All Black, he slipped a sweet pass to winger Teddy Morgan.

The howls of the fans were so loud they could be heard for miles around. With his ears ringing, Morgan raced over and scored! The training session from earlier in the week had paid off. The Dragons had bamboozled the All Blacks and led 3-0. But could they hold on?

Desperate New Zealand came at Wales harder than ever. But no matter how powerfully they charged or how fast they moved, a man in a red shirt would just get a hand to a Kiwi boot or grab a fingerful of black jersey. Someone, somehow, always did just enough to spoil the attack and halt the previously unstoppable scoring machine.

But then – disaster! Late on, a New Zealander called Bob Deans crashed through a tired tackler. The green grass of the Arms Park seemed to open up and he appeared certain to score. Looking to make the conversion easier for his team, he swerved towards the posts. As if from nowhere, a red shirt appeared and Deans crashed to the floor. Centre Rhys Gabe – who had never given up the chase, no matter how hopeless it had seemed and how much his lungs burnt – brought him down inches short. The crowd held its breath as Deans twisted and writhed towards the line. PEEP! The referee blew his whistle... and... and...

"No try!" proclaimed the official. "He wriggled to the line. Penalty to Wales!"

Cardiff Arms Park exploded with joy and relief. Just minutes remained. Were Wales about to pull off their most famous win yet?

Minutes later, with Mr Nicholls still bravely leading the way, Wales made their final defensive stand. New Zealand, truly desperate now, tried again and again but just couldn't break the iron defence. After another formidable Welsh tackle, a Kiwi fumbled the ball near the Welsh line. Mr Nicholls gathered it at his toes, evaded several wild tackles and booted the ball off the park.

The referee checked his watch and then blew his whistle.

50,000 voices exploded as one! Pandemonium! 'Gallant Little Wales' had shocked the world. Thousands of hats and leeks were thrown into the air as people hugged, danced and cried tears of joy. Mr Nicholls, a true gentleman and leader, ran straight over to the devastated All Blacks to shake hands and tell them how much he admired their incredible rugby skills and fighting spirit.

As the crowd sang hymns and the aching and bruised Welsh players listened proudly, Mr Nicholls exchanged his scarlet shirt for the black one of his opposing captain, Dave Gallaher. No two athletes ever respected each other more than those two great men did at that moment.

With songs of praise rising in the winter air, the warriors departed the field and walked into history. The All Blacks played 35 games on that 1905 tour and lost only this once. In total, they scored an astonishing 976 points and gave up just 59. So epic was the battle that cold December day, people still talk about it in awe well over 100 years later. It is claimed by some that on his deathbed, Bob Deans – whose try had been disallowed – whispered, "I did score at Cardiff!"

Mr Nicholls is still remembered by all proud Welsh rugby folk and the iron gates that guard today's Cardiff Arms Park bear his name. Each generation of Welsh people continues to relate the story of the time the mighty All Blacks first came to Wales and how Mr Nicholls showed that they were human after all.

Through hard work, clever thinking, inspiring leadership and brave play, the 'Prince' returned to the field of Welsh dreams and took his country to the top of the rugby world.

ACKNOWLEDGEMENTS

I wish to express my sincere thanks to all the kind folk at Y Lolfa for making this book happen.

The professionalism and enthusiasm of Carolyn Hodges, my editor, has been infectious. She has been a delight to work with. Similarly, my thanks to Lefi Gruffudd for championing this idea and Ceri Jones for all his hard work on the design.

My eternal gratitude to the magnificent illustrator, Carys Feehan. To work on a book with my 'little niece' has been a huge source of pride and I'm honoured to have my words sit alongside her inspired images.

I am indebted to my true rugby hero, my father, for helping review the book in its early stages. He was always a role model to me on the field and continues to be one for me off it. My ever-supportive wife Helena must be thanked profusely for (again) allowing me to retreat to my desk and spend countless hours 'living' with rugby players who hung up their boots over a century ago.

Finally, thanks to the men of 1905, whose deeds ring through the ages and have fired my imagination since I first read about them as a young boy. I hope this book can play a part in keeping their deserved legend alive. Perhaps the tale will inspire some young readers to one day equal the glory won in those distant days and once more place Wales atop the rugby world.

James Stafford
October 2021